MONEY QUEEN

A Simple Financial Framework For Soulful
Entrepreneurs To Run A Profitable Business
While Living A Fuller Life

Bridgette Boucha

MONEY QUEEN

A Simple Financial Framework For Soulful Entrepreneurs To Run A Profitable Business While Living A Fuller Life

Bridgette Boucha

Copyright © 2023 - Reflek Publishing

All Rights Reserved.

No part of this publication may be reproduced, distributed, or transmitted in any form or by any means, including photocopying, recording, or other electronic or mechanical methods, without the prior written permission of the publisher, except in the case of brief quotations embodied in critical reviews and certain other noncommercial uses permitted by copyright law.

Disclaimer: The author makes no guarantees concerning the level of success you may experience by following the advice and strategies contained in this book, and you accept the risk that results will differ for each individual. The purpose of this book is to educate, entertain, and inspire.

For more information: hello@unicrowns.com

ISBN Paperback: 978-1-7378283-6-5
ISBN Ebook: 978-1-7378283-5-8

This book is dedicated to the entrepreneur who is enthusiastically committed to growth, service, mission, abundance, and most importantly . . .
JOY.

FREE GIFT
Fit for a QUEEN

As a huge thank-you for choosing this book, here is a bonus gift to get you started on your profitable business and fuller life today!

MONEY QUEEN MODEL:

Some of the free resources in this book include:

- 5 Ways to Become More Profitable
- 5 Ways to Improve Cash Flow
- $500K Offer Calculator
- 3 Pricing Strategies You Can't Live Without
- How to Get 5 Hours of Your Time Back Each Week
- Your very own customized Money Rituals checklist
- And more!

MONEY QUEEN MODEL

Get your free gifts here:

https://bit.ly/moneyqueenresources

Contents

Preface ix

Introduction 1

Part 1: Relationship with Money 5

    Chapter 1: Money Story 7

    Chapter 2: Money Selves 15

    Chapter 3: Money, Reframed 23

Part 2: The Four R's 35

    Chapter 4: Rainbows 37

    Chapter 5: Revenue 49

    Chapter 6: Resources 61

    Chapter 7: Rituals 93

What to Do Next 99

Acknowledgments 101

Would Love to Hear From You! 105

Preface

My heart was pounding and my hands were shaking as I approached the door. This wasn't my first time, but I knew it would be my last.

It was the Monday after Thanksgiving in 2015 when I decided to turn in my final resignation to leave the structure and stability of the corporate world.

Maybe you're like me and have felt trapped in a life that isn't yours. For high achievers like us, it's often deeply rooted in how we define success, and it starts from an early age.

I grew up in Minnesota. My dad was a hockey player. My mom, a nurse. They divorced just a couple months after I was born, so at just three years old, I started splitting summers and holidays traveling between two very different households. There was often an element of unpredictability and uncertainty. I knew early on that my adversity was not going to define me; I was going to create a path out and define myself.

That path was my career path, and it was pretty clear to me from the beginning. By *clear*, I mean I had a simple conversation with my Gum (grandmother) that went something like this:

Gum: Bridgette, what is your favorite subject in school?

Me: Math.

Gum: You should be an accountant.

Me: Okay.

Like many of you, I was told that the key to success started with a solid education and ended with a stable job. Accountants were a safe choice in that they were always in demand and had the potential to make good money.

So, naturally, I went all in on this plan. Accounting degree, corporate job, relocate for the corporate job, CPA license, and ultimately . . . CFO. Chief Financial Officer! Friends, I was thirty years old, and I had arrived! Success was mine. Everyone was proud of this accomplishment, but most importantly, I was proud. You couldn't wipe the smile off my face. I had done all the right things, and this was my reward. My path led me here. I loved it.

From the smiley receptionist who greeted me each morning to the smell of coffee brewing as I walked powerfully in my stilettos and pencil skirt toward my beautiful private office filled with important documents and laced with purpose. Yeah . . . I loved it.

Until that smile started to feel robotic. Like this success I had been seeking no longer felt like success. The company didn't change; I changed. Something inside me started to feel disconnected, frustrated, confused . . . trapped. If this was everything I ever wanted, why was it no longer enough?

After resigning, I took some time to silence my environment so I could ask myself questions like *What would success look like for me today?* and *How would it make me feel?*

Well . . . do you know what happens when you get silent?

The outside voices disappear, and the inside voices get louder. And these are not the RA-RA voices. These bitches came to play. Doubt, fear, shame. I quickly began to realize I had zero idea who I was without that CFO title. My success was tied to something I was willing to let go of. It's like the path turned into a moving walkway and I was rapidly picking up speed while my life was passing me by. I didn't feel defined. I felt confused, lost, and ashamed. Somewhere in the midst of chasing success, I had completely forgotten who I was.

Becoming an entrepreneur was my chance to reclaim my life and build a business that brought me money, joy, abundance, and a level of success that felt good to me.

Except, that's not how my story unfolded.

Almost nothing about my early experiences of entrepreneurship brought me what I was looking for. To be honest, I had no idea what I was doing. Being a corporate CFO did very little to prepare me for entrepreneurship. I was playing really small. Overdelivering and undercharging. Had no boundaries. Money was tight. I didn't enjoy my work. I felt unsupported and alone. I cried . . . a lot. Surely, this was not the life I had envisioned when I left my corporate job.

Sometimes, your path is clear from the beginning, and other times, it unveils itself when you're feeling most vulnerable.

In 2019, I joined my first mastermind. For those new to the concept, a mastermind is a small to medium group of people who share the same values or have similar goals. The purpose is to provide mentorship, peer support, brainstorm ideas, and offer a safe space for the roller coaster of emotions that come along with entrepreneurship.

The investment of $8K felt like a huge stretch, but I saw no other way. Up until this point, I had been entrepreneuring on my own. I had no idea communities and resources like this existed, but I did know that what I was doing had not been working.

Within a month of registering, I found myself at our first in-person event, in a room with fifty of the most passionate entrepreneurs. I knew I needed to be in this room, but when I got there, uncertainty settled in.

Did I belong here? These people are magnetic. Funny, confident, vibrant. There was a light about them. They were so excited to ideate and share about their businesses. Like you, these entrepreneurs were eager to learn. Fully committed to growth, personally and professionally. Deeply connected to mentorship and community. While I was committed to these too, I felt extremely intimidated to be in their presence. I knew I had to show up for myself and for my investment, so after some inner pep-talks, I bucked up and started having conversations.

As I leaned in to learn more about these fascinating humans, I heard them share about their products and services, their marketing funnels and their team. They told me about their clients, their families and their travels. There was an undeniable excitement and glimmer in their eyes as they spoke their hopes and dreams into existence. The vibe was high, and I was feeling beyond inspired and fortunate to be in such great energy.

And then, like a switch, things changed.

When I asked them about their finances, they froze. One by one. It was as if the light and energy drained from their faces right before my very eyes. There was a sense of overwhelm and a feeling of fear and shame. Many said this would be the year they would get their financial shit together. Others avoided the topic entirely.

I watched their passion turn into pain. I saw their abundance turn to avoidance. I became fearful for them and their mission.

These people were incredible. Larger than life in my eyes. And yet, there was a giant piece of their puzzle missing, and it happened to be the only piece I held.

I immediately understood the reason I was there. I could learn so much from them! And them? They needed a safe space to talk about the one thing that could literally make or break their business: MONEY.

I built my entire career around numbers, and this was my chance to give back.

You are probably wondering how a book like this can simplify something that feels so complex.

Rest easy. Your guide has arrived. And I'm giving you all the goods. Who am I? I am the one who is fiercely committed to reducing your learning curve by providing you a soulful, practical approach to managing your finances. A framework that begins with you and ends with you. I teach it because I live it.

Introduction

As an entrepreneur, you understand sacrifice. You know what's at stake if your business doesn't survive through the year.

Maybe you also left the stability of a steady job and are trying to prove to yourself, and perhaps others, that this decision to start a business was a good one.

Maybe your emotions around money are stifling the energy you desire to put out into the world through your products and services.

Maybe you realize that obsessing over everything in your business besides your money is a short-term strategy, but you, my friend, are ready for the long game.

Only 50 percent of new businesses survive beyond five years.[1] In fact, in the hundreds of entrepreneurs I have served, several of them started off ignoring their finances favoring the following strategies:

---

[1] Maryam Mohsin, "10 Small Business Statistics You Need to Know for 2023," Oberlo blog, Oberlo.com, January 28, 2023, https://www.oberlo.com/blog/small-business-statistics#:~:text=As%20a%20matter%20of%20fact,from%20starting%20your%20own%20business.

"I've got money in my bank account, so . . . I'm good!"

"Credit cards still work. Success!"

"Made it this far without financials, so I must be doing something right."

"My numbers drain my energy, so not looking at them is best for my business."

Does this dialogue sound familiar? Of course it does. You picked up a book about financial empowerment, which tells me something about you.

YOU are ready to elevate your experience.

YOU are willing to learn and implement.

YOU are about to change your life and business.

I LOVE you for it!

Who are my clients? Oh, they are amazing humans just like you. Mission-driven, heart-centered, product- or service-based entrepreneurs who value community, are committed to personal growth, and are determined to leave people better than how they found them. If you are a client of mine reading this, shout-out to YOU for taking ownership and responsibility of your money. If you've never heard of me before you picked up this book, get ready. Your life is about to change. Perhaps not overnight, but most definitely over time.

There are a ton of books out there about money mindset and manifestation that leave you feeling inspired about money. Too many financial strategies fail to take YOU into consideration. Your life is not a transaction.

It's time to figure out what really matters to you—beyond any sexy "success" metrics we often see on social media. Maybe you don't want three homes, four cars, and a yacht. Maybe you prefer to take several trips a year, dropping into different cultures, eating amazing cuisine, and exploring the world with an open, curious, and loving lens. Okay, that one is me to a tee! No matter what version of life feels best to you, it's important that your financial framework and strategy support it.

This book is a lovely combination of logic and magic. I believe you need a little of both, and I'm here to share exactly how I have used numbers as my superpower and how you can too.

Now that you know what this book is, I can assure you what this book is not. Nobody, including me, is trying to make you an accountant. Bless the souls who love the spreadsheets, but damn, if that is not you, I honor that.

So what can you expect in this book?

We're going to start with your money story. We've all got one! Your financial footprint is as unique as your DNA. You can't change your DNA, but you can change your money story and it's critical that we start there because like anything that grows, it starts at the root.

After that, we'll squash some of those fears that keep you up at night. We'll address the limiting beliefs that can keep you feeling stuck. Nothing about waiting will ever make you more worthy than you are today. Let that one land as you sit up a little taller, understanding that you are beginning a journey of financial empowerment and making an investment that, when utilized, will pay you back for the rest of your life. How 'bout that ROI!

From there, we'll get into some *really* fun stuff: what you truly want out of life. Not the things that look good on social or that you think would make others proud or envious of you. I mean the real-deal shit. The deepest, soul-filling, biggest, juiciest life you can possibly imagine. Why? Because when we move into your business, it must support the lifestyle that makes your heart smile or else what the hell is it all for?

Then come the actions. A step-by-step guide to building sound financial practices. We'll cover key areas like revenue and pricing. You'll know exactly which numbers you need to look at on a weekly and monthly basis. You will understand HOW to optimize your most important resources: time, people, money (hey-o!), and energy. Like I said, part logic, part magic. You'll receive tips to increase profitability—you are a for-profit business, yeah?

Finally, you'll walk away with new rituals designed to help you integrate aligned financial strategies to produce both money and joy into your life.

Let's get started!

> "Not what we have but what we enjoy, constitutes our abundance." —Epicurus

Part 1

Relationship with Money

We *all* have experiences that shape who we are, what we believe, and how we see the world. But just because something is shaped doesn't mean it cannot be reshaped. For some of you, it might just take a little massaging in order to experience changes. For others, it may require a deeper look, way down to the root, to see where your beliefs began to grow. This concept of reshaping applies to many things, but for this chapter, we are applying it to one of the primary reasons you picked up this book in the first place: you want to improve your relationship with money.

CHAPTER 1
Money Story

"Your reality is created by what you focus on and how you choose to interpret it." —Jen Sincero

We *all* have a money story. How money makes us feel. Our relationship with money. What qualities we assume about someone who has money. How we treat money when we have it. The language we use when discussing it, if we even discuss it at all. How has our money story been shaped? Here are a few common contributors to get you thinking about yours.

1. Upbringing. How was money spoken about in your household?
2. Personal experience. How have you treated money since you began earning it?
3. Peers. What kind of money mindset do the people you spend time with have?

Upbringing: The Tale of Two Households

When I was growing up, bouncing between a single mom household and a dad/stepmom household, I experienced two different views about money.

My mom was a prime example of a woman who could work, earn, and provide for her family no matter the circumstance. She worked evenings as a registered nurse on the oncology floor of a hospital. While money had to have been tight back then, owning a townhouse, raising two kids by herself, and working full-time, we didn't ever feel that. Mom made sure the house was neat and clean and the fridge was stocked. She is irritatingly responsible when it comes to punctuality. She pays bills early (gah . . . a tip I will tell you NOT to do later), balances her checkbook (google it, Millennials), is habitually first to volunteer to work overtime and double-pay holidays. She prioritized saving for my college and developed a good relationship with her banker so that if/when the time came to leverage debt, she was in a good position to ask. While she didn't speak about money from a place of scarcity, she did make sure the money she spent on us was for us. New school clothes? Yep, but they were meant for me and only me, not to be swapped with friends as so many girls do in school. There are a million things I appreciate about my mom and how she exemplified financial independence and responsibility for me at such an early age. And while she has been so many positive things to me and to the world, there is one thing she has never been . . . an entrepreneur.

Dad, on the other hand, led a completely different life, and my time spent with him growing up gave me a host of different perspectives around life, money, and responsibility. As early as seven years old, I started spending summers with him in a small town in northern MN, just six miles from the Canadian border in a town called Warroad, population 1,200. He was born and raised there to very humble beginnings, one of nine children living in a two-bedroom home that had flooring placed over a dirt floor. His dad, my grandfather, was a commercial fisherman in Canada where he met my dad's mom, my grandmother Alice, who grew up on the Animakee Wa Zhing reservation and was raised by her grandmother, known as Laughing Mary. Gosh, if I could only meet the woman who was given this nickname!

It was identified early on that Dad was a gifted athlete. While he didn't have the financial resources, he did have the talent and the backing of a small town who had produced several Olympians. Coming out of Warroad, also known as Hockeytown, USA, he experienced massive opportunities beginning with state high school hockey notoriety, a silver medal finish in the 1972 Olympics, and a professional hockey career including accolades such as Detroit Redwings Rookie of the Year and a place in the United States Hockey Hall of Fame. With a devastating eye injury at just twenty-four years old, his professional career was cut short with little to fall back on.

While I wasn't born when this occurred, I did experience the wake and destruction of such a life-altering experience. Dad had an entrepreneurial spirit, creating his own hours selling real estate, making appearances at several events in support of the hockey community, publishing a book, and public speaking. Money wasn't readily available or handed out. I had chores and could earn money by mowing the lawn (still love the smell of fresh-cut grass to this day) and helping my stepmom clean some local establishments. When I joined her to clean the local bar at the liquor store, I was able to keep any loose change I found underneath the barstools. Earning money became important to me during these years, so at just thirteen years old, I rollerbladed to my first ever interview at a local restaurant, and while it took me a few rounds to figure out what the fuck I was doing, I did become obsessed with my growing tip jar. If I worked more, I earned more. And earning money gave me options.

The culmination of my upbringing helped to shape my money story even though I didn't realize it at the time. While neither of my parents managed money for a living, we all in fact manage money for a living.

My mom showed me how a woman can be financially independent by taking full ownership and responsibility for her financial situation and being hyper-aware of her earning and spending.

My dad showed me that, even at a young age, you can work to earn. Whether it be household chores or slinging breakfast plates, working resulted in money, and money resulted in choices. While he, admittedly, isn't the best at managing money, he found ways to generate money after a massive career change he never saw coming.

It is said that our attitudes, beliefs, and emotions about finances form by the age of seven years old.[2]

Think about your upbringing and what experiences might be shaping your money story today.

Personal Experience

Your personal experience with money is the direct result of how you have implemented your money story into everyday life.

Think of your very first paycheck. How did you feel and what did you do with that money?

Do you have a credit card? Benefits, points, miles, cash back? Debt, interest?

Are you a saver? Does money feel better to you in a safe space tucked away for a rainy day?

Or are you more of a spender? Forget the rainy day, you want to make it rain ALL day!

Do you view money as a short-term tool or a long-term tool?

As a business owner, your personal experience with money gets amplified. Where you once were responsible for only you, there is now more at stake. People are watching. Your friends, your family, your peers, your social media following. The decisions you make

---

[2] Brent Weiss, "Your Money Mindset Forms by Seven: And the Gift Keeps on Giving," Kiplinger, Kiplinger.com, January 18, 2023, https://www.kiplinger.com/personal-finance/your-money-mindset-affects-financial-decisions-for-a-lifetime.

impact the longevity of your business and can sometimes feel like a hundred-pound weight has been added to each decision. Top that with the constant pressure to *look* like a successful business.

Got news for you: the difference between looking like you have a successful business and actually having a successful business is not dependent upon positive thinking or positive posting; it's in positive cash flow.

Whether you feel you've made good or bad financial decisions in life, you carry that with you into business ownership. When you know better, you can do better. Before you're too hard on yourself, there is no shame in the story you have today. Luckily, personal experiences can be replaced with *new* personal experiences. And with the tools in this book, they will be.

Peers

What are people saying or not saying about money around you?

When I left my corporate career, I felt completely isolated. My friends and family were all working in more traditional structures, meaning they worked for someone else and had a steady paycheck, health insurance, and likely some sort of commute. I, on the other hand, had willingly abandoned such structure and stability in exchange for the pursuit of something I couldn't even describe at the time. I trusted that my inner knowing had bigger plans and I wasn't about to abandon her.

Yet, my conversations didn't foster a space for abundance and prosperity that exceeded a traditional salary. The narrative I held onto was that success resulted in burnout.

In fact, the first contract CFO job I took, I undercharged because a recruiter told me that I would never get $135/hour. I asked for $100/hour and ended up compromising to $80/hour. What the actual fuck. My reality around my worth was shaped by the people I surrounded myself with. Many of us undervalue ourselves, especially early on because we don't understand how to price; we feel unworthy of our value and lack confidence in communicating it to our clients. My second engagement, I charged $195/hour and, from that point forward, stopped charging by the hour entirely. If you're not in the presence of others who think, speak, and act with understanding of this concept, you run the risk of undervaluing, undercharging, and resenting your work. Instead, surround yourself with expansive thinkers, incredible doers, and massive supporters.

Identifying your money story:

- What are some contributions from your upbringing that have shaped your money story?
- Do you believe these contributions to be true and inspiring or untrue and limiting?
- What emotions come up for you when you think about money?
- When you receive money, are you more of a "save it for a rainy day" or a "make it rain now" kind of person?
- How is money spoken about, if at all, in your closest relationships?
- If today you started a new relationship with money, what would it look and feel like?

Remember, your money story is as unique as your DNA with one critical difference: you can't change your DNA, but you can change your money story. Understanding your relationship to money will help you create solid financial practices that will change your conversation around money from one that may be in a place of fear or shame to one that represents potential and possibility!

CHAPTER 2
Money Selves

"The events of your past are fixed. The meaning of your past is not." —James Clear

Money is a renewable resource. Time is not. And yet, the connection between these two incredible currencies is electric. Like time has a past, present, and future, your money does as well.

Let's use points in time to define your money selves. Past money self accumulated all of your experiences with money prior to today. Current money self is you *now,* reading this book so you can identify and implement changes. Future money self is who you are becoming as a result of your decisions. Each money self is important to your journey. Let's walk through each one a bit deeper.

Past Money Self

This is you and every way you have handled money up until this point . . . your personal experiences from the prior chapter.

Perhaps you've gotten yourself into (and perhaps out of) debt.

Maybe you made investments in items that you later regretted. Who hasn't?!

Possibly, you've found yourself penny-pinching when you thought for sure you had made it past that by now.

Your past money self should not be shamed; she should be celebrated! Without this valuable experience, you would have nothing to build on. Your past exists to teach you something. If avoided, you'll continue to create situations designed to teach you the same lesson.

In college, I was terrible with money. I worked a few hours a week in my Native American Studies library but nothing that would support the money I was spending on partying. Even with cheap college drinks (25 cent tap beers? [Gag!]). This was back in the day of checkbooks where if you wrote a check and didn't have enough money in the account, you would get an NSF (non-sufficient funds) notice and fee. I think the fee was around $35 per check but don't recall the exact amount. What I do recall is the day my mom found a box of paperwork I kept from college and found all the NSF notifications. I could have vomited right there. Not only did I waste her money to cover the fees, but I also felt reckless about how I was handling money. Mind you, I was getting my degree in accounting, so add that layer of shame to my spiral and it was a rough go. How could I be so irresponsible? The shame stung enough for me to change my behavior.

The summer before my senior year in college, I got a highly coveted intern position at a great company that paid well. Realizing I could make good money made me want to take better care of it. Any careless fees due to poor cash flow management would be coming out of my pocket. That alone was enough for me to start monitoring my money and watching it grow. Remember that loose change I got to keep from cleaning the bar? And that tip jar I loved to watch grow? This was like that but next level.

From coins to dolla dolla bills! And beyond that, I wanted to create opportunities for myself. I knew pissing my money away would not allow for that to happen. I'm thankful for my past money self for teaching me those lessons.

Whatever goals you have, money can help you get there.

Want to build generational wealth? Managed money can multiply for years to come.

Have a deep desire for philanthropy and charity? Donated money goes way further than donated time.

Looking to change your environment or living situation? It takes money to make moves.

Want to inspire others with your stories of transformation and growth? People are watching. These humans deserve to see an example of a strong, independent, financially empowered rockstar in their life. *You* get to be that person by putting in the work to improve your money story.

What has your past money self illustrated for you?

Here are some prompts that may help you:

- How have I used money to enhance my life?
- How have I used money in ways that might make me look happy but not feel happy?
- Have I ever been in debt, and if so, does that pattern continue?

Now that you have identified some major contributors to your past money self, you can see how those experiences might still show up today in your life and business. In turn, you can identify how to make changes to support your current money self.

Current Money Self

There is no time like the present. If only we could all live there in real time! Many people feel stuck in the past because they haven't taken the time to acknowledge, accept, and act on lessons they've been provided. This is a huge waste of valuable experience! If you don't use it, what was it all for?

Here are some questions to get you started.

- Does my bank account activity align with what I value?
- If not, what void am I trying to fill with these purchases/investments? (Hint: Belonging or instant gratification may be big ones.)
- As a business owner, do I feel confident in my financial decisions?
- Am I using my numbers as a tool for accountability and growth?

- What behaviors from my past money self still show up in practice today?
- What exact emotions (be specific) am I looking to shift around money?

Tip: If you're feeling stuck, write down what you don't want and allow the opposite to become more clear.

Example:

Don't want: I no longer want my money to be a mystery. It causes me stress and anxiety. I wake up wondering if I'm going to be "okay."

Do want: I want to learn my numbers so I can feel clear about my finances, reduce stress, and improve my sleep knowing exactly what I need to do to reach my goals.

No matter what you discovered about your past money self, you are now acquiring the tools to make improvements. The combination of your newfound knowledge and the tools in this book will have you loving up on your current money self.

Today is the day you start a new relationship with money. You *get* to decide this. You are the source. You create the life you desire. Today and every damn day moving forward. Will you be the most perfect financial specimen that ever existed? Nah, perfection isn't what we are after. This book is for the people who embody and embrace progress, and progress leads to financial empowerment.

Progress generates momentum.

Momentum creates consistency.

Consistency produces results.

Results build confidence.

Confidence is the baseline for your financial empowerment. The higher the baseline, the faster you rise from it.

To illustrate, when you drop into a bucket of fear or shame, as we all do from time to time, it's not about avoiding it altogether, it's about not going as deep and not staying as long. We are spending this valuable time together so we can raise your baseline and lift you out of the bucket faster.

Future Money Self

You are actively building the foundation for a more prosperous, abundant, aligned you.

What would it feel like to understand and use your numbers to create the life and business you desire?

How would you walk into a room differently if you felt financially empowered to speak about money?

What actions can you take today to prepare for your future money self?

That is the version of you who:

- takes ownership of your financial situation—past, present and future
- practices soulful money rituals to stay in tune and accountable to your financial strategies
- understands that in creating financial structures, you create financial freedom
- becomes nimble during financial uncertainty to better stay relevant and in service

Life comes at you. The economic environment is all over the place, unpredictable at best. The news is fear-based clickbait. And yet here you are, your very own most valuable asset. Educating and empowering yourself to take ownership of your financial situation. Your past money self is in awe of your newfound commitment. Your current money self is feeling proud of every shift. Your future money self is doing fucking cartwheels because you took the time to make intentional changes with how you handle your money.

Learn from your past money self.

Commit to your current money self.

Create your future money self.

CHAPTER 3
Money, Reframed

"Don't let money run your life, let money help you run your life better." —John Rampton

When you were a kid, money meant you could buy *fun* things! You may not have worried or even wondered where the money came from. You just knew that when given the chance to pick a toy or buy a snack, money was the way you could make that happen. As your world expanded, so did your understanding of money.

Maybe you got your first job and deposited your paycheck into your account. Or maybe you blew the whole thing on fun things! And then you got your second paycheck and wanted to see the money grow. But, as you got bigger, so did your toys. Phones, clothes, cars, travel. You began to see how earning money and buying things were related. Perhaps even thought, *I had to work a whole month to pay for that new purse,* and it made you stop and think for a minute, even if you bought it anyway. Or maybe you got credit cards and thought they were the greatest thing on the planet until you realized how long you had to work to cover the minimum payment and, worse yet, interest payments.

Money began to feel more complicated. Less about fun and more about fear.

As a business owner, you understand how often fear shows up. You are continuously putting yourself out there for all the world to see. Hello, judgment! You are working on solutions to problems, building relationships, managing a team, and developing your personal brand all the livelong day. Some days success is simply not giving up.

For many of you, money is one of your primary fears when it comes to business. How long will it last? Am I going to be okay? Can I afford that?

For *all* of you, money is one of your most important resources because without money, you have no business.

We do all this work in personal development to ensure that we have a solid inner foundation: mind, body, and soul. Yet, the fear around money doesn't get the love and attention it deserves.

So it seems the perfect time to go into the common fears around money so you can truly understand how this beautiful resource is a tool of abundance rather than a symbol of scarcity.

Here are some common fears around money that are limiting your potential.[3]

---

[3] T. Harv Eker, "10 Limiting Beliefs Around Money Preventing You From Success & Wealth [Infographic]," Million Dollar Life Lessons, Harveker.com, accessed

"Money is a limited resource."

I remember the first time I heard the phrase, "You can create money out of thin air." My initial response was automatic: "Yeah right, easy for rich people to say." (Hellooooo, money story.)

My past money self had only experienced earning money in exchange for hours worked. In other words: here is your job description, fulfill it and we'll pay you a salary, perhaps a bonus, and give you a 3 percent annual merit raise if you don't fuck up. There was nothing that came out of thin air.

Yet, other entrepreneurs were creating it and showing me what was possible. The entrepreneurial energy was completely different from anything I had ever known. You don't just dream bigger and think differently, but you do the damn thing.

I quickly began to see how each one of us has gifts and can use our businesses as the vehicle to deliver those gifts. We create solutions to problems that exist in the world and therefore create money for ourselves, seemingly . . . out of thin air.

When you can solve someone's problem with your expertise, there is value in that, and you deserve to be paid. People are spending money to get what they want and need. What on earth would make you think that your gift could not make that list?

Limiting belief: Money is a limited resource.

Reframe: Money, like your potential, is unlimited.

June 15, 2023, https://www.harveker.com/blog/10-limiting-beliefs-on-money-infographic/.

"Too many people are doing what I do so I can't earn money."

Hear me . . . what makes you credible is not what makes you incredible.

Credible

Things like your degree, resume, work experience, the letters behind your name. The shit you put on LinkedIn that groups you into a pool of people with your same credentials.

Incredible

Your voice, your style, your personal experiences, the way you solve a problem, how you make people feel, the very essence of who you are. Credibility is fabulous but by itself is a disservice to your unique gifts. Sit down or stand out. The choice is yours!

I'm a fractional CFO, Chief Financial Officer. A quick google search on "find a fractional CFO" turned up 362,000 results in .52 seconds. At first glance, this could feel debilitating for me. But instead, I'm going to tell you two reasons why this empowers me:

1. My services are in demand! People need fractional CFOs *and* they are searching for them. There were five million businesses started in 2022 (up 42% from pre-pandemic times).[4] You know what every single one of those businesses

---

[4] Luke Pardue, "Census Bureau Data Confirms Surge in 2022 New Business Applications," Gusto Company News, Gusto.com, January 17, 2023,

will ultimately need to survive? Financial strategy and support provided by a CFO. If I don't put myself out there, they'll never find me. What a shame!

2. Like rainbows, no two humans are alike. My personal experiences, professional background, and unique voice allow me to connect with people who relate to my style of service. I love to speak about energy. I deeply desire to understand the human behind the business owner. I am known to drop an f-bomb while feeling either excited or upset. My mission is to support you and tell you the truth so you can make more aligned financial decisions. Not every business owner wants this style of service, and I'm grateful for that because it makes room for the ones who do.

People are out there solving problems you also know how to solve. Fantastic! Just means that your solutions are in demand. There is someone out there struggling because they haven't found YOU yet. Wave your weird flag so your people can find you.

Limiting belief: Too many people are doing what I do so I can't earn money doing it.

Reframe: My industry needs me, and there is more than enough opportunity for everyone.

---

https://gusto.com/company-news/2022-new-business-surge-census-data#:~:text=There%20were%205.0%20million%20new,right%20to%20start%20a%20business.

"More money, more problems."

Think of all the things that matter to you in your life. Now think of all the ways money could help you improve them.

Money is a universal exchange. You can earn it, spend it, give it away, invest it, save it. Sure, there are some real dickheads out there who use money in ways that your kind-hearted, mission-driven soul wouldn't dream of. Power and greed are not part of the formula of this book. This book is about helping you improve your money story and implement sound, soulful financial practices. If after that you become a dick, that's on you!

In 2009, I got a divorce and told myself I was going to be financially independent for the rest of my life. I hired a financial advisor and told him I wanted to retire at forty-five years old, or at least make work optional. He didn't laugh at this declaration of mine so I believed it could be true. Smart man. I shoved money away into investments, maxed out my 401K, and kept a healthy amount in my bank account. I went to Mexico a few times a year with friends to all-inclusive resorts and made my way up to MN to visit family each year. Then plans changed, as they often do, and I left corporate and my ability to save more money for a while. But the money was still there, growing and doing its thing on my behalf.

So when the opportunity came up to invest in a mastermind, I knew this was how I would fund it.

Past money self (the saver) took care of current money self (the dreamer) so that future money self (the doer) could embark on the most exciting, expansive, and transcendent chapter of her life to date.

Money allowed that to happen.

Before we go further, I must tell you that every financial situation is different. I am certainly not suggesting you do what I did, but merely allowing you to see how money gives you choices, and with those choices, you can create opportunities to live a better life, as defined by you.

The concept of money being used in various ways is a testament to its versatility. It's like tofu taking on the flavor of the dish it accompanies. Money takes on *your* flavor so you can amplify your mission.

Like most people, I have had money and I have not had money. Money was never the problem. It was the meaning I assigned to it.

When I was working my ass off in corporate, I had more money than I had ever had before, but I had no time to spend it or enjoy it. So one weekend, after years of over-achieving, over-delivering, and over-justifying, I took myself to Tiffany's. Yes, you know the place. I left with three little blue boxes wrapped in perfect white ribbons with bows on top. I waltzed out of that store much like I waltzed into my corporate office: powerfully. I texted a pic to my now husband and posted on Facebook as if to show the world that I was happy and successful. I needed instant gratification. Something tangible to make me feel whole where I felt empty.

That was eleven years ago. And what I realize now and every time FB reminds me of that memory is that success cannot be seen. Success is a *feeling*. Only you can describe it.

These days, instead of scrambling to find an hour on the weekend to buy myself something nice, I spend time traveling the world. Part solo, part social, pure joy. My definition of success includes experiences that make me feel alive and connected. I now buy myself things because it makes me *feel* happy, not just look happy.

Once I got clear about what truly mattered to me, I began to use money as a tool to live the life I felt I deserved.

Limiting belief: More money, more problems.

Reframe: More money, more solutions.

"I'm not worthy of having money, wealth, or abundance."

Ouch, right? Deep wound. A worthiness wound is a real thing.[5]

It's a deeply held belief that we are in some way inadequate, less than, or broken. Its origins lie deep in our childhoods, where we were likely made to feel inadequate and unworthy. These wounds show up in more ways than just money: happiness, love, authenticity, belonging.

---

[5] Above The Middle, "What Are Worthiness Wounds?" Illumination, Medium.com, May 4, 2023, https://medium.com/illumination/what-are-worthiness-wounds-e8fc627b67c9.

Any self-sabotagers out there? I can relate. For as long as I can remember, my mind has been a warehouse facility for memories that don't serve my highest good. I believe if you're reading this you may have a facility of your own. When things are good—I mean really good, in life, love, and business—you might find yourself sneaking into this warehouse, looking through the pallets of stories that represent your deepest insecurities as if to remind yourself that you are unworthy of happiness and good fortune.

When things appear to be too good, you go and mess them up. When things get quiet, you get loud.

It's like that time you met someone and in an effort to appear funny or cool, you said something completely out of character and immediately wanted to retract it but instead found yourself trying to cover it up with more words. Not more words! Yes, more words. And while that person is entitled to form their own opinion of you, you also form an opinion of yourself about this exact exchange and punish yourself . . . forever.

If you can relate, then you certainly agree that this energy is not going to generate the abundance you seek.

Here are some steps designed to help you feel more worthy.

1. Identify your strengths. It is 100% likely that you are good at something that someone else is not. You might not recognize it as your superpower because what comes easily to you is not your pain point. But it is someone else's.

2. Set goals. Create what I call snack-sized strategies so you can reach more milestones that result in quick wins.
3. Practice self-care. Do things that make you feel good and allow you time to reboot. Self-care goes beyond spa days, but don't forget those either.
4. Surround yourself with positive people. People make a huge difference in your outlook based on their energy, topics of conversation, and level of support.
5. Be kind to yourself. Humanize the journey to self-development and give yourself grace. "Entrepreneurship is a personal growth engine, disguised as a business pursuit."[6]

Limiting belief: I'm not worthy of having money, wealth, or abundance.

Reframe: I was born worthy.

"I am not good with numbers."

Look, I've always loved math, numbers, and spreadsheets, so I'm going to turn this one over to real-life transformations from my clients to help show you what is possible here. See for yourself!

Client 1:

Female seven-figure business owner knew absolutely nothing about her numbers. Her husband (at the time) handled her business

---

[6] James Clear, "3-2-1: Entrepreneurship, habits, and the joy of climbing," JamesClear.com, May 14, 2020, https://jamesclear.com/3-2-1/may-14-2020.

finances and told her she wasn't good with money and didn't understand her finances, which she believed for many years. After she got divorced, she hired us to help her set a financial framework and design a financial strategy so she could develop knowledge and independence with her money. She has since been able to increase her profit, work less hours, max out her financial investments, and confidently speak about her financial situation. The shifts go well beyond financial knowledge. Her leadership style, communication, boundaries, and confidence continue to evolve!

Client 2:

Female seven-figure business owner had a terrible experience with a prior CFO and was determined to run her business using her intuition as her guide, because, well, it had gotten her this far. After hiring a financial advisor to begin building her personal wealth, she quickly realized that she had to start with the source: her business. She hired us to help build a plan that better suited her ideal lifestyle. With a plug-and-play cash flow model, a new outlook on finances, and the team in place to support her hundreds of ideas (love my creatives!), she now uses her money map and cash flow tools to plan ahead, make decisions, price profitably, and set monthly targets so she can use both her intuition (magic) and her numbers (logic) to fulfill her mission.

Limiting belief: I am not good with numbers.

Reframe: I am learning my numbers.

Look, we all have fear. Fear of heights, fear of public speaking, fear of snakes, fear of failure. Fear is a commonality among all humans.

Sometimes fear is good because it keeps us safe. Other times fear limits us from our true potential. Example, you're on a stage speaking in front of a crowd and you experience fear. You're not likely afraid because someone is going to jump up on stage and physically harm you. You're more likely afraid that the audience is going to judge you. Your body does not know the difference. If you let that fear take over, you might limit your potential for delivering a phenomenal message to your incredible audience.

The goal is not to go through life without experiencing fear. It's to overcome the fear that holds us back from our true potential.

Part 2

The Four R's

Let's get into the how! The process of creating a financial strategy for a profitable business while living a fuller life can be broken down into four R's:

Rainbows, Revenue, Resources, and Rituals.

Something as simple as this cannot be scary. In fact, this is exactly where it gets exciting! You are not doing this alone. I am about to walk you through each R and provide the step-by-step exercises so you can complete this process in real time.

There is only one promise I want you to make to yourself before moving forward.

Repeat the following phrase. Say it loud. Say it often!

I promise to allow myself to play.

You are creating a framework for the life and business that feels most abundant to you. Play with it! Think outside any social norm and release the inevitable possibility that someone may judge you for it. Nobody else's input is more valuable than your own.

Like you and like me, this process is part logic, part magic.

Let's roll!

CHAPTER 4
Rainbows

"As she let go of the adventures not meant for her, she was brought new ones aligned with her magic."
—Spirit Daughter

The first step in this process has nothing to do with numbers. Money is just one currency. We need to consider time, joy, energy, and fun. Your life deserves your attention. How can you possibly use money to build the life you feel you deserve if you aren't clear about what that life is?

Take for instance, a rainbow.

A rainbow represents many things to many people including hope, beauty after a storm, diversity and inclusion, a pot of gold, a positive shift in vibration, or simply a sign of happiness and health. What an incredible symbol. The science behind it will also tell you this:

No two people see the exact same rainbow.[7]

The rainbow in this process represents your fuller life. You are the only one who can see it, so you are the only one who can describe it.

Perhaps the most important part about this process is that your definition of a fuller life can and will evolve as you do.

You may recall my story about feeling trapped in a life that wasn't mine. When I was just twenty years old, I joined corporate America as an intern. I quickly realized there was a hierarchy of success defined by the corporate ladder. I'd look at my bosses in their private offices with their important meetings and confidential paperwork and think how much I wanted to reach that level. My goal quickly became clear. Top of the org chart! C-level kind of shit. Every step I took during this season of my life was to get me closer to that rainbow. I worked weekends. I relocated for my job. I volunteered for projects. I created relationships that resulted in opportunities. And after fifteen years of climbing and clenching to that top rung of the ladder, the pot of gold at the end of the rainbow no longer felt like a reward.

Redefining what you have known to be true for yourself may feel confusing at the time, but you evolve. Your decisions should evolve as well.

What looks good on paper doesn't always feel good in purpose.

You can go find a ton of resources about building and scaling a

---

[7] "Rainbow," National Geographic Resource, NationalGeographic.org, updated March 17, 2023, https://education.nationalgeographic.org/resource/rainbow/.

business, but they fail to take one very important thing into consideration: your fuller life.

Have you ever admired someone from afar and wished that you could have their life? Yet, in reality, you may not be willing to sacrifice what it would take to have it. I always think of six-pack abs to put it in perspective. While they look amazing and I'd love to have them, I have not prioritized the lifestyle it would take for me to get them. Translation: wine and french fries always win.

Your business is no different. There are sacrifices that are made in order to start, grow, and scale a business that not everyone is willing to make. That is why entrepreneurs make up 16% of the adult workforce.[8] It's not for everyone! But here you are, part of the 16% who are ready and willing to work hard to build what you want. And thankfully, because of this book, you will do it with your fuller life at the center.

Setting up a business that doesn't support how you want to live can leave you feeling out of alignment, burned out, and eventually resentful of the very thing you have created.

So before I show you how to define your fuller life, I must address a very unfortunate, yet very common, pitfall to be aware of.

Comparison. There is no shortage of examples out there for business owners to spiral out about. Know that anyone out there who you admire is just as human as you. Everyone is trying to do

---

[8] "Entrepreneur Statistics," ThinkImpact.com, accessed June 15, 2023, https://www.thinkimpact.com/entrepreneur-statistics/.

the best they can with the tools they have. You are not meant to connect with everyone. Not everyone is going to love you. Release that expectation and build the damn life you feel proud of, no matter what it looks like to someone else.

Remind yourself that external validation will only bring you short-term significance.

While I love to feel motivated and inspired by what others are building, I have admittedly gotten caught up in the hype before. Thoughts like this can easily enter your mind:

"I should be doing that strategy. I am not doing enough on social media. I should be further along in my business. I really do need that purse. I don't have enough [insert phrase here]."

Give yourself a quick cleanse from comparison. The next time you scroll, ask yourself this:

Is my feed feeding my soul? Remove anything that doesn't inspire or entertain you. You've got better things on the horizon. Like defining your rainbow.

As a CFO for business owners, I help you get clear about what success feels like first so we can build the business around that. If you're going to flip your life upside down, like many of us do when we start a business, you better build it back the way you want it.

That is exactly why every financial strategy needs to start with you. I can build you any kind of business plan, but if it doesn't ultimately light your soul on fire and support the lifestyle you envision for yourself, it is total crap.

Defining your fuller life.

We are going to use two exercises to help you define your fuller life: PCV and FMB as defined below.

PVC: **Personal Core Values** are your fundamental beliefs and highest priorities that drive your behavior.[9]

FMB: **Feel My Best** is a list that includes specific activities that when included in your day to day, bring out the best you and create the most joy.

Let's get to it:

Step 1: Personal Core Values

Our personal core values help us connect to our authentic selves and provide a greater sense of purpose. They drive our behaviors, shape our personalities, help in decision-making and goal-setting, and ultimately determine what actions we take in life. Understanding our PCV gives us a better understanding of who we are at our core.

When asked about creating the sculpture of David, Michelangelo said,

---

[9] Logan Hailey, "Core Values List: The Only 216 Values You'll Ever Need," Science of People, accessed June 15, 2023, https://www.scienceofpeople.com/core-values/.

"I created a vision of David in my mind and simply carved away everything that was not David."[10]

Imagine if you carved away all that wasn't you. What core beliefs would direct you in living your fuller life?

Remember your personal core values are *personal* in that you get to determine what they are. Here is a list of common PCVs to get your wheels turning.

Integrity	Honesty	Patience
Creativity	Loyalty	Excellence
Courage	Kindness	Justice
Leadership	Trust	Wisdom
Respect	Freedom	Innovation
Compassion	Determination	Curiosity
Accountability	Authenticity	Fairness
Humility	Spirituality	Independence
Diligence	Generosity	Perseverance
Listening	Patience	Self-Respect
Collaboration	Connection	Discipline
	Growth	Gratitude

---

[10] Good Reads, Michelangelo Buonarroti Quotes: https://www.goodreads.com/author/quotes/182763.Michelangelo_Buonarroti?page=2

Six tips for identifying your PCV:[11]

1. Think of your favorite memories. What made them so meaningful?
2. Think of your least favorite memories. What made them less meaningful?
3. What kind of stories inspire you? This says a lot about what you value.
4. What kind of behaviors make you angry? This allows you to see what you don't want and choose the opposite.
5. Imagine your ideal world. How would people interact and treat others?
6. Review the accomplishments you're most proud of. What about them made you feel proud?

Here are some of my Personal Core Values:

Curiosity	Perseverance
Freedom	Gratitude
Connection	Fun!
Accountability	

I incorporate these into my life through the choices I make. What I pursue, the relationships I nurture, how I spend my time.

Curiosity: I love learning and incorporate it some way into my every day. Listening to a podcast, making meaningful connections

---

[11] Elizabeth Perry, "20 personal values examples to help you find your own," BetterUp blog, BetterUp.com, June 7, 2022, https://www.betterup.com/blog/personal-values-examples.

with new people, watching documentaries, and reading nonfiction books. Listening and observing.

Connection: Nurturing relationships with people who support, inspire, and challenge me. Meeting new people and having meaningful conversations.

Freedom: Flexible scheduling and boundaries allow me to create more freedom in my life related to time. My business provides me more financial freedom because as a business owner, I have unlimited income potential.

Accountability: So much accountability! I have accountability partners, my running group, my book coach, my communities who help me stick to my goals.

Perseverance: I love achieving goals. From checking things off a list to running marathons to writing this book.

Gratitude: Having a gratitude practice has absolutely changed my energy. Seeing the good in myself, others, and situations has brought more good into my life.

FUN: A simple question I ask myself often is, *How can I make this more fun?* Oftentimes, I can and I do!

Your turn! Make a list of your PCVs.

I always recommend you set the space for a fun exercise like this. Cozy up with your favorite bevvy, light a candle, play some music, open a window, burn some sage, do some you. If you're not in a place to do so, a simple voice note or a Google Sheet from the airport sky club also works fabulously. In other words, your life doesn't need to wait until you find the perfect spot to get started.

Step 2: Feel My Best List

This one is really fun and excitingly specific to you. This list provides you with a menu of things to pick from when you're planning your week or looking to infuse some joy into your life. How great is that? Trust me . . . you're going to be thrilled that you've taken the steps to better understand what feels really good to you without all the extra noise. Time well spent!

Examples (can be anything, one thing, or several things, your choice):

Moving my body
Daily thirty-minute walk, train for a competition/marathon/race, become certified in yoga, stretch for five minutes every day.

Getting into nature
Start each day with five minutes outside, go on walk and talks with friends, find a local park to run/walk/read in.

Good, quality sleep
Set a night routine that fosters a good night sleep like Brendon Burchard's 3-2-1:[12] no food three hours before bed, no work two hours before bed, no screens one hour before bed.

Designated time with family

---

[12] Brendon Burchard, "Sleep Better: My Evening Routine," Brendon Burchard.com, December 7, 2019, https://brendon.com/blog/my-evening-routine/.

Call your parent(s) once a week, plan a family trip, do Sunday dinners, set a game night no-phone rule to facilitate more convos.

Unlimited travel
Determine your travel bucket list and get to planning.

Faith
Completely individual. Decide what faith means to you and how you want to incorporate it into your life.

Reading
Pick your next book to read and set time. Certain # pages, certain # hours, join a book club, start a book club, or just read according to your desires.

Writing
Got a book on your heart like I did? Take the next best step. Research, hire a mentor, set a schedule, and make it happen.

Solitude (OMG, how I love thee)
Take a solo trip. Take yourself on a date. Take time to yourself, even if you are just relaxing with your thoughts. Get to know yourself better without all the influence of others.

Positive impact to others

Volunteer, teach

Personal development

Financial stability and growth

Upcoming events:
Wedding, anniversary, trip, time off.

Your turn! Build your Feel My Best (FMB) list now.

This list is fluid and evolving. While your PCV may not change much, some of the activities on your FMB list will. It's best to review this periodically so you can recalibrate when needed.

Once you gain clarity about what is important to you (PCV) and how you want to spend your time (FMB), you will be better equipped to actually make this your reality.

Congrats! You have laid the foundation for the rest of the process. We are going to refer back to these resources later in the book to make sure the only rainbow you're chasing is your own.

PCV + FMB = fuller life!

CHAPTER 5
Revenue

Can we get a slow hand clap for revenue please? Friends, you can look like you have a business or you can actually have a business. The difference is whether people are paying you.

Revenue, revenue, revenue. This book alone will not provide you with a profitable business. In order to apply the framework, you have to be generating revenue. In order to manage money, you have to have it in the first place.

This may surprise you . . . or not? My most consistent question I ask on client calls is this:

What are you doing to generate revenue?

That's right, folks, hear me when I say: **When in doubt, generate revenue.**

It seems simple and obvious that income-producing activities would be on your list of priorities, yet many of us find other ways to spend our time.

For the entrepreneurs scaling to multi-six- and seven-figure annual revenue, you are likely the face of the brand. You are on your social media platforms, taking discovery calls, closing sales, and delivering the product or service. Yet, somehow your calendar gets filled with non-revenue-generating activities. I get caught up in this too and understand how you feel when something more exciting pops up to distract you. And yet, we must remember that your entire financial strategy is contingent upon you having money.

Look, each one of you has a gift. How you deliver it into the world is determined by what offers you put out there. You have identified what matters to you (PCV) and how you choose to spend your time (FMB), now let's zero in on your **offers**.

Think ahead to the next twelve months. How can people work with you? Understanding your offers will help you get really clear about how to lay out the rest of your year. Every entrepreneur I have ever worked with wants this kind of clarity. You are about to have it.

Will your plan change? Probably! The environment and demands of your clients are ever-evolving. You're getting feedback every day. You need to be nimble, but being nimble from a solid foundation will help you make changes and *still* reach your personal, professional, and financial goals. How 'bout that!?

Let's begin building the foundation. We'll use a funnel concept that goes from free to high-ticket offers and typically is for service-based businesses.

Put your party pants on and get ready to think about offers in these buckets:

Free

Free offers should require less of your energy, minimal cost to you, and zero cost to your audience.

How are you entertaining, educating, and establishing credibility? People buy from people. Allow them to get to know you and everything you can bring to the table. The goal is to expand your reach and grow your audience with people who need what you have to offer.

Examples of freebies include social media content, blogs, video, lead generators, podcast interviews, unpaid speaking/guest coaching, email newsletters, workshops, etc. Several of these *can* be monetized, but for this purpose, I'm talking the value you give away for free.

Low

Low-ticket offers are your lowest priced (besides free, of course!). They require energy on your part and allow the audience to take what they've learned and implement it themselves. DIY, do-it-yourself model.

These are often designed for you to serve a larger group using less of your time. A one-hour workshop with fifty people, for example. You teach something, and it is up to the client to take it from there. They are responsible for execution. Other examples include virtual workshops, masterclasses, collaborations, memberships, or even a book like this one. Low-ticket offers should always include a CTA (call-to-action) so your audience knows exactly how to continue working with you at a higher level.

Medium

Medium-ticket offers are the next step from low-ticket offers and typically require more direct involvement from you. More of a DWY, do-it-with-you model.

Similar to the low-ticket, these can be group formatted, and they promise a bigger transformation. Higher value, longer duration, perhaps an in-person event or retreat. The experience is elevated, and the price point reflects that.

High

High-ticket offers are the most expensive way to work with you. They are high touch, high value, and require more of your time and energy. They are exclusive and usually limited to a certain amount that you can offer in a given time period in order to protect your time, energy, and capacity.

These are typically one-on-one experiences or non-group. Private coaching or providing ongoing services to a client. In my business, this offer is our Money Mapping Experience followed by our ongoing monthly services of CFO strategy and monthly bookkeeping. Learn more about Money Mapping at www.bridgetteboucha.com. Paid speaking can also go into this category. This high-ticket offer is likely where all your other offers lead into.

You may not have offers in every category today, but it's important to look at what you offer in these buckets so you can better answer the following questions:

- How are people finding you?
- How can people work with you at different price points?
- What journey are you taking them on to reach various transformations?
- Do you have upsell opportunities and strategies for them?
- Can you create recurring revenue streams with your offers?

Let's put some numbers to it!

Say you have the following three offers for the next twelve months with the targets below.

Offer #1 (High): VIP Strategy Sessions, $15,000, 1 per month, ramping up to 3 per month

Offer #2 (Low): Membership, $99/month, 20 members, ramping to 75 members

Offer #3 (High): Paid Speaking, $10,000 per event, 3 events per year

Would you believe it if I told you the above model would result in $500,000 in annual revenue? It's true. Sometimes you need to simplify in order to scale.

Go to https://bit.ly/moneyqueenresources and grab my free $500K Offer Calculator and plug and play all you want.

I used to have a large variety of offerings in my business. Money is the modality with which I serve, and being that almost every adult in the

US uses money on a daily basis, there are plenty of directions I could go. During the pandemic, I pivoted until I got dizzy. Then, I landed. Once I simplified my offerings and identified my signature offer, the Money Mapping Experience, everything changed. My life got easier, my offers were in alignment (free, low, medium, high), and my business grew. I was able to streamline everything from marketing to onboarding, which in turn resulted in more revenue generated.

Niche down. You can always add later.

Now, before I ask you to make a list of your offers, I need to address a common place where entrepreneurs get hung up. Pricing.

Pricing

Pricing your offers tends to bring up all kinds of emotions. Impostor syndrome, unworthiness, scarcity, uncertainty. In reality, pricing is key to profitability. It's not what you sell it for, it's what you get to keep, so understanding your costs + value is critical to the longevity of your business.

In fact, underpricing hurts your business in three very particular ways:

1. You are unable to cover your costs.
2. Potential clients perceive cheaper as lower quality.
3. Unequal energy exchange can create resentment.

If you are like many people who struggle with pricing, this section was designed for you. We're going to dig into pricing in three ways: value, relativity, and increases.

Value

Cost + Value = Price

Defining value can feel tricky because there is not always going to be some tangible input, like a cost, but trust me when I say it must be considered.

In other words, it's not simply the number of hours it takes you or the amount you pay your contractors for the job but also the power of the transformation that you are providing.

If you are doing any of the following for your client, you are providing massive value.

- Reducing their learning curve
- Giving them their time back
- Educating them with knowledge they can use forever
- Empowering them with confidence to level up
- Giving them access to your network or community

You are solving problems, and you deserve to be paid for that. It may have taken you years to acquire the skill sets and experience you have today, not to mention the financial investment. There is value in that!

Let's also consider the pain points of the clients you serve.

How big is their pain point?

Maybe you are in operations and set up systems and SOPs (standard operating procedures) for business owners. They may be leaving money on the table because they don't have workflows to turn client deliverables quickly and accurately. They are frustrated doing the admin work and recreating the wheel with every new client onboarding.

Leaving money on the table? Frustrated? Pretty big pain points.

What is it worth to them to have this problem solved?

Using the example above, if the proper systems and workflows were in place, how much time and energy could they get back? Relief, trust, better sleep, less anxiety? Massive pain point.

Pain points translate to value once *solved*.

What is the long-term value of the solution you're providing?

Same example: Does this new SOP allow them to onboard at least one more client per month, therefore increasing revenue and enhancing client experience, which then improves reputation? Now that is some serious VALUE!! As our friend Rory Vaden says, "Reputation precedes revenue."

Remember this formula: Cost + Value = Price

Consider what you are providing to your client and what they are gaining from working with you to help you quantify value. If you don't believe in your value, the client won't either. Take time to get clear and confident on the value you provide, and include it into your pricing without hesitation. Once you secure an offer at your new rate, you'll never unsee it. You are always only one client away from confidence in a new price point.

Relativity

When you price your offers, they should make sense relative to one another. Meaning, the more involved you are, the higher the price. A group program should be less of an investment than working with you one on one. Like any rule of thumb, there can be exceptions. For example, if you have a live event coming up and just want to build an audience to get hype before the tickets are on sale, you may give a TON of value in a free or low-ticket workshop in order to turn around and sell the higher-ticket event. Pricing can and should be used as a strategy.

A few pricing strategies to consider related to relativity:

Anchor Pricing: Providing options allows potential clients a point of comparison. They can see prices relative to one another. If I gave you one price of $5,000, you might think that's high. But if you know the other options are $8,000 or $15,000 and can see the value associated with each, you now have a point of comparison that will allow you to better understand which option is best for you.

Floor Pricing: Everyone should have a minimum amount to charge. I also call this your walk-away point. No matter the scope of work, there is a certain level of time, money, and energy involved. Use accounting, for instance. Oftentimes we have to do the same amount of work whether a client is making money or losing money. In fact, we have to do more when a client is losing money due to extra reporting and strategies around cash flow. Make sure you have an energetic and a monetary floor in place so you can easily make decisions and understand your walk-away point.

Early Bird Pricing: You've all seen this. Offering a reduced price for those who commit during a certain period of time before the price goes up. This can work really well, but I also encourage you to consider adding a bonus versus a discount to keep your profit margins up. Bonuses can be something you've already created from low-ticket offers or even a bonus group call with you. Still, early bird pricing is a great strategy to encourage enrollment.

Increases

How do you know when it's time to increase your prices? Here are some scenarios where you should consider it:

Your costs have increased.

You are incredibly lower than services similar to yours.

You are reaching 80 percent capacity.

You are introducing a new offer (a.k.a. new price point) or relaunching an old one.

You haven't increased in the last twelve months.

Now, I hear this all the time. If I raise my prices, I will lose my audience. You either have an audience issue or an efficiency issue. See below.

1. Audience Issue: Maybe you have the wrong audience and need to get in front of people who not only see the value that you provide but can afford to pay for it.

2. Efficiency Issue: If the market you're in will not sustain a price increase, you have to figure out a way to do it cheaper. Automate and delegate. There are so many entrepreneurial-friendly systems and resources (freelancers/contractors) out there designed to streamline your processes and potentially reduce your costs.

Communicating a price increase can also feel scary, but I'm here to tell you that it is a necessary part of running a business. You are no good to anybody if you're broke.

When communicating a price increase, consider the following:

- The timeframe. Give them notice of sixty to ninety days so they can plan ahead.
- Communicate, don't convince. This is not a negotiation unless you make it one.
- Transparency is key. If the scope has evolved into more work for you, the price needs to match.
- Send it with love and excitement, and continue serving them at the level they deserve.

Also important, not all price increases need an announcement. You can start proposing to new clients at your new price point for all engagements after a certain date. Your existing clients may be grandfathered in at your current rate until some of the scenarios above have been met.

Whew! Let's take a moment to breathe. Inhale peace, exhale love.

You're building the framework for your next twelve months by using some very intentional, heart-centered tools. Now that we've gone through offers and pricing, it's time to start planning yours.

Make a list of what you plan to offer for the next twelve months.

Once completed, grab your PCV and FMB and ask yourself this question: *Do my offers align with my personal core values and allow me space for my Feel My Best list?*

I can give you ten reasons why answering that question is important, but you only need one: You are building your business plan around your lifestyle plan and not the other way around.

CHAPTER 6
Resources

"Snowflakes are one of nature's most fragile things, but just look at what they can do when they stick together."
—Vesta M. Kelly

When I first became an entrepreneur, I felt alone. Unaware that communities existed especially for people like me, I isolated myself thinking that I had to learn, do, and achieve everything on my own. Seems silly to write about that now, knowing the incredible amount of resources available to people like me and you. But back then, I didn't know what I didn't know. If you're writing the story of your life and business but you can't see what's even possible, you end up limiting yourself by what you believe to be true. For me, that meant I was playing very small and trying to do everything on my own. I had left a career where I was responsible for managing large teams and wanted absolutely no part in that moving forward. I had been known to jokingly say, "I used to be a people person, until people ruined it." That mentality not only kept me small but created a very lonely journey in the beginning. Thankfully, I now know that does not have to be the case for me, for you, or for anyone willing to build a business from the ground up. We have people and we are most definitely stronger together.

No matter what kind of business you own, you have some very critical resources at your fingertips. By the end of this section, you will have actionable ways to optimize each one of them. I get so excited to talk about these because these strategies have helped me improve my life in ways well beyond my business because, well, it's all connected. Treating life and business separately at this stage may leave you feeling exhausted. The energy you put into your life and your business come from the same source: you. For many years, my career got all my good juju. My life got whatever was left over, if anything. So backward, yet so common.

There are four resources I believe to be most critical in your business. They are energy, time, people, and of course... money. These resources, when optimized, can help you create the wildest version of success, abundance, and joy you can even imagine. Success, of course, being solely defined by you. Remember, not everyone wants a 10X'd business with a multi-seven-figure exit, and you shouldn't feel one ounce of guilt whether you do or do not. Think about your rainbow! No matter where your life, business, and goals stand today, you can and will benefit from the pot of gold I'm about to share with you.

Energy

Thissssss one. You guys, lean in for this first resource.

Have you ever tried to run on fumes?

Lack of sleep, lack of clarity, lack of patience.

It is so important that we take inventory of our energy so we can show up at the frequency needed in all areas of our lives, not just the business. Gone are the days of business as usual. Welcome to the days of preserving, leveraging, and capitalizing on your energy.

During the pandemic, our lives were given an elimination diet. Social interactions were banned. Events were canceled. Travel was grounded. Commitments were excused with no explanation needed. Your calendar was cleared for almost everything except things you could do from home or within the parameters of distancing and curfews. It was nuts! *And* one of the greatest opportunities to get super intentional about what you added back to your life. For the first time, possibly ever, you got the chance to see what it felt like to actually get your time back.

Many people created new structures of boundaries after experiencing the pandemic. Others couldn't wait to get back to "normal," and so they added people, activities, and commitments back without much consideration of how they truly felt about them.

No matter where you fall in the above, I invite you to re-evaluate now. Your fuller life depends on it. And I'm going to show you exactly how!

Friends, I introduce you to the Calendar Review. It's fun, it's simple, it's free, and it's *powerful*. I started doing this ritual in 2019, and the results have been profound. My life has improved, but more specifically, I experience more joy, set stronger boundaries, allow grace, learn by my own examples, celebrate the shifts, and recalibrate often. Are you ready?

Grab a pen and paper and open your calendar.

This exercise assumes that you are like me, someone who lives and dies by their calendar and puts everything into it. If your life schedule lives in another place, open whatever you use to keep yourself on track.

Exercise: Calendar Review, Energy +/-

Draw a line down the center of the page. On the left, write Energy+. On the right, write Energy–. Grab the free worksheet at https://bit.ly/moneyqueenresources and print as many copies as you need throughout the years.

Next, you are going to go through each event in your calendar for the prior period (week, month, quarter, year—you choose!) and write it in one of these two columns. As always, feel free to put your own spin on this ritual to make it your own.

Energy+: This column is for calendar events that gave you energy. Maybe it produced laughter and filled your soul. Maybe it produced income and filled your bank account. Maybe it did both! Things in this column are things you want more of and intend to repeat in some way, shape, or form. Celebrate these!

Energy–: This column is for calendar events that drained your energy. An obligation you said yes to, but you really wanted to say no. A meeting with someone who wasn't in alignment with you or your mission. There is no shame in this column, but rather acknowledgment so that if/when the opportunity comes up again, you may choose differently.

As mentioned, you can do this for any period of time you'd like. I look back to the prior week, month, or quarter and always do a full annual review in January. Yes, even if you do this practice throughout the year, it is still helpful to do a full twelve months to kick off the new year in alignment. Regardless, choose what feels best to you and just get started!

The benefits of this practice are plenty. Here are just a few examples of how to use your calendar as a cross-check for your goals below:

Do you want to grow revenue but barely have time dedicated to this goal?

Is fitness part of your FMB list, but there is no time set aside to work on it?

Did you declare family time as a PCV yet you're taking meetings during dinner time and on weekends?

Have you set a goal to write a book but not allocated focused writing time to get the words from your head onto paper?

Your calendar should be an exciting documentation of the life and business you're building. And because this book is part logic and part magic, I must include room for the magic in your calendar.

The Importance of White Space

White space is unscheduled time. It's time you intentionally set aside or may unintentionally get back if someone has to reschedule a meeting. Both are gifts that leave room for magic.

Here are a few ways I use white space to my advantage.

Processing time. No back-to-back calls, if I can help it. I need time to prep before a call and time to process after a call. White space is critical for me here. Do you have time in between appointments or are you jam-packed frantically trying to shift gears from one to the next. Frantic isn't a good look on anyone. Do yourself a favor and add some buffers so you can properly download from one activity before diving into the next.

Break times. In writing this book, I set my timer for fifty minutes and went hard on writing until the timer went off. Then I took a move break. Could be a short walk, a dance party, a snack, a laundry folding sesh, or anything that got me up and freed my body/mind from the writing position. It allowed me focused time to write, and fifty minutes didn't feel overwhelming. I then got a mind and body break to shake up some energy before the next round if I was repeating the cycle. If not, I got fifty minutes in full flow mode, which can result in around a thousand words written. Break times force you to be more efficient and productive for shorter periods of time. Game changing!

Opportunity time. If your calendar is packed to the gills, there is no time for you to seize an opportunity you didn't see coming. Look, we're all placing orders with the Universe every single day between our content, connections, and conversations. When that opportunity arises for you, you want to be able to explore it without moving around a bunch of commitments. And if today isn't the day that opportunity arises, then you have built-in time to pick something from your FMB list. Win-win.

This calendar exercise brings a heightened sense of awareness to the areas you want to *avoid* going forward. Writing something on your Energy− column is like anchoring in a feeling that you will recognize when/if that feeling comes up again. You will make decisions that better align with your energy as a result of this very practice. How cool is that?

When I started my Calendar Review rituals back in 2019, my Energy− list was way longer than my Energy+. Over time, it has thankfully, happily, and gratefully shifted so that the Energy+ columns are longer, indicating a fuller life by my definition. This isn't to say things don't creep in, and sometimes I may fall back into old ways from time to time, but the practice of reviewing and holding myself accountable often reduces my chances of working on other people's agendas instead of my own health, happiness, and abundance.

How to Use Your Calendar Review in Life and Business Alignment

Refer back to your offers for the next twelve months. These offers have provided you monthly targets. What activities will help you reach those goals? Are they in your calendar?

Simply put, if you want to reach your goals, you must prioritize the activities it will take to get you there.

Time

The most important currency of our lives! It's precious, non-renewable, and something we all have at this moment, but there's no guarantee as to how long it will last. We often get reminded of the fragility of this limited resource when tragedy strikes but tend to fall back into patterns of people pleasing and overcommitting too easily.

How would your life improve if you could get five hours back each week? I have just the exercise for you.

Exercise: Time Tally

What tasks show up on your list from week to week?

Start a list today and add to it for the next week or so to capture the many things that you are responsible for. Important: These tasks should include everything, not just business. From grocery shopping to dog walking to cleaning your house to giving a speech. All of it lives here. The less time you have available to run your profitable business and live your fuller life, the less chances you have of achieving it.

Thankfully, there are resources for almost anything these days. You're not bougie if you have someone to help you with everyday life, you're resourceful. And you need to be.

The goal here is not to overwhelm you but to empower you. After completing this exercise, you will clearly see where you have opportunities to get some relief through the use of resources.

Three steps to complete a Time Tally

Step 1: Make a list of tasks. Break it down into steps, if applicable.

Step 2: For each one, list who owns the task (you as primary or someone else).

Step 3: Categorize each of them into one of the following:

- Automate – You can invest in a software system or create a workflow to streamline this.
- Delegate – You can assign this to a team member or *future* team member.
- Eliminate – This task is not a priority or no longer in alignment and needs to be shed. Bye!
- Keep – This is a task that only you can do, you love to do, and that brings you money or joy.

Let's talk about some examples for each of these:

Automate

Anything related to client experience or onboarding, call scheduling, project management, ordering supplies or groceries, automatic bill pay setup, electronic invoicing/ACH drafts, password security software, even setting your coffee to brew in the morning! Look for repeatable tasks, not the one-off ones, and create systems to streamline. We are so fortunate to live in a world with plenty of options to automate. Explore them!

Automation client win: We set up electronic invoicing and bill payments for a client so they could better manage their cash flow.

Many entrepreneurs struggle with inconsistent cash flow so here is a quick pro tip on cash flow management:

- Receive money faster
- Pay out money slower (not late, not early, but when *due*)

Delegate

Things you are doing that someone else could *easily* pick up for you. You wouldn't delegate something like giving a speech, but you certainly could delegate a spreadsheet project or admin work. You could also delegate errands, grocery shopping, house cleaning, dog walking, lead generation, marketing services, graphic design, transactional work, project management, and even shopping/styling your wardrobe. Somebody out there does exactly what you need and likely enjoys doing it. Offer them a chance to make money while helping you. Win-win!

Personal win: I recently brought in someone to help me streamline my client onboarding process. This process was a perfect candidate for both delegation and automation because it was . . .

- Repeatable, which means we could create workflows and use systems without having to recreate the wheel each time.
- Not specific to my skill set, which means I wasn't the one who had to or was most skilled to set it up.

Eliminate

Trust me when I say you are doing something today that you don't need to be doing at all. Maybe you implemented a process way back in the day, but it no longer applies to this season of your business. When your business model evolves, your offers change, and your resources must also be reevaluated for relevancy. Maybe you joined a group and you are no longer seeing a benefit or just flat out don't enjoy it. Get rid of it. Now is the time to set massive boundaries.

Personal win: When I first left corporate, I diversified myself into a frenzy. For years, I held onto hosting my online fitness groups even though it had nothing to do with my fractional CFO services. I still use the products today and have accountability in other ways, but I do not need to put the time and energy required into running the groups because my focus is on financial education and empowerment at the global level. Simplify in order to scale.

Keep

These are the things that live in your zone of genius. Only you can do them or you want to do them because it lights you up that much! Your "keep list" may vary depending on your role in the company and season of business, but I'm betting if I ask you your favorite part of running your business, you could complete this sentence today: "I would be so happy if I could do [this task] all day, every day in my business and the rest was handled."

For me in my business today, I *love* to do the following: client financial strategy calls, in-person Money Mapping Experiences, speaking on stages, guest coaching, recording content (and then handing it off to my marketing team). Sure, I still have some tasks to offload, but there are a lot less than there used to be thanks to this exact exercise.

I believe you deserve the same kind of clarity and relief. Bringing visibility and accountability to how you're spending your time will allow you to see areas where you can shed those five hours a week. Maybe it's an hour a day or maybe it's five hours in one shot. Hint: Look at how much time you spend in meetings. Reducing any sixty-minute meetings to thirty- or forty-five-minute meetings is a great place to start.

Money is renewable, time is not. Spend wisely!

People

You are the most valuable asset in your business and the people you surround yourself with affect your potential.[13]

I always say numbers are my jam, but people are my GOLD. What I mean by this statement is that when I went from an isolated entrepreneur to one who surrounded herself with wonderful people, everything changed for the better. My inner circle is not large, by design, but my network of amazing humans is growing. Here are some ways these relationships show up in my life and therefore impact my business.

---

[13] Ann Y.T. Chui, "The Hidden Power of Every Single Person Around You," LifeHack, LifeHack.com, updated February 14, 2023, https://www.lifehack.org/634714/the-hidden-power-of-every-single-person-around-you.

Mentors: People I have hired, worked with/for, been in communities with, or just admired from afar. These are people I support and seek guidance from, either formally or informally. Having mentors in place is a game changer for any entrepreneur. Being in the energy of expansive conversations and massive accountability allows you to rise up to levels you may not have otherwise considered possible.

Peers: My biggest gift from joining masterminds has been the relationships that have come out of them. You aren't going to click with everyone and, hear me when I say, you don't need to. It's the relationships you willingly nurture after the paid container closes that is the gift that keeps on giving. When you go through transformations with others, it creates bonds of unwavering love, support, and friendship. Some of the people I feel most close to today came from mastermind experiences, and I'm forever grateful I said yes to those opportunities.

Strategic Partners: I always say 1 + 1 = 5! When you collaborate with others who have complementary services, the value goes way UP! Identifying people to partner with, whether it's a collaboration or affiliate situation, can create large trajectories of growth for everyone involved.

Groups: Oh my, find a group you have something in common with and watch your world change. For me, this is my workout and running groups. The accountability is enough on its own, but the friendships I have built over the past decade have been priceless. You really get to know each other when you're on a long run and cannot be distracted by your phone. No matter what you're into, I can assure you that someone else is into it too. Go find them!

Friends: This one goes wide. We all have friends from different eras of our lives. A close-knit group from high school, a crew of college besties, an "I met you as an adult but feel like I've known you forever" type, etc. These friends are in your life for a reason, and while it may not be to help you scale your business and build your dreams, it is certainly something to cherish as long as it still feels good to you.

Family: The ones you can't choose! Just like any group, you don't have to click with everyone, even if it feels like you are supposed to. Sharing DNA does not require you to like someone. Regardless of your family situation, know that those who truly love and support you will always want you to succeed.

Take a look at the above categories and do a quick inventory of your people. Ask yourself these questions:

Mentors: Who are my mentors and why?

Peers: Who are my go-to people to talk to about life, business, and entrepreneurship?

Strategic Partners: Who am I currently partnering/collaborating with? Who would I love to partner/collaborate with?

Group: What am I interested in? Do I have a community that supports it?

Friends: Are my current friendships a representation of my past, present, or future? Can be any combo, but be mindful of your energy with each commitment.

Family: You do you on this one!

If who you spend your time with affects your potential then this exercise is *priceless*.

Refer back to your latest Calendar Review. Check that Energy-column for names and you'll easily be able to see where you can make improvements and set better boundaries for future months. And yeah . . . congrats on getting that energy back, queen.

As a business owner, you may have noticed one very important group of people I haven't addressed yet. Your team.

I heard this somewhere and think of it often: "If your dreams don't involve other people, they aren't big enough."

When your business is becoming bigger than you, it's time to invest in people to join your team. It can feel scary at first. Maybe you're afraid to let someone peek behind the curtain because it's such a mess. Or perhaps you're worried about being able to afford them long-term. Whatever fear might be holding you back, know that with the right support, you can create a bigger impact and get some of your time back if these are some of your goals.

You can hire people for myriad reasons. Here are a few below:

- Professional expertise, guidance, compliance—accounting, legal, insurance

- To give you your time back—operations, assistants, integrators
- To sell/promote on your behalf—marketing, sales, affiliates
- To fill a gap in your skillset—insert weakness here (we all have some!)

After working with hundreds of scaling entrepreneurs, here are some of my top tips to consider when adding team members:

Start on a contract/project basis for ninety days. This allows each of you a chance to work together before you have a full-time commitment and reduces the expenses associated with full-time hires such as payroll taxes, benefits, etc. Try before you buy.

Be extremely mindful when hiring friends or family. I didn't say don't do it, I said to be mindful. Meaning, you must set very clear expectations and boundaries. Communicate often and quickly to make sure everyone stays on track. Respect each other and your roles within the company. When hiring family and friends works out, it can be one of your biggest competitive advantages. If it doesn't work out, more than your relationship may be at stake. It may impact your company, reputation, and other team members. Not to mention, it totally fucks up Thanksgiving.

Set new team members up for success. They should be able to answer the following questions:

- What are my responsibilities?
- How will my performance be measured?

- What are the company goals for the next ninety days? Annually?
- How do I contribute to reaching the company goals?
- What is the preferred method and frequency to communicate to my manager? Team members?

If you can't answer these questions, they won't be able to either. As Brené Brown says, "Clear is kind. Unclear is unkind".[14]

Money

Let's keep it simple! As a business owner, there are five key numbers you need to know, track, and improve in order to run a profitable business. I'm going to break them down below.

1. Revenue

You have already read a whole chapter about revenue and pricing. Consider yourself ahead of schedule, but do not skip the rest of the goodies below.

What it is:

Revenue is also known as income or gross sales. It is the lifeline of your business because it indicates that people are not only interested in but buying your product or service.

---

[14] "The 45 Best Brené Brown Quotes About Courage, Shame & Vulnerability," Four Minute Books, FourMinuteBook.com, accessed June 15, 2023, https://fourminutebooks.com/brene-brown-quotes/.

Why revenue is important:

- If you don't have revenue, you don't have a business.
- Revenue dictates or justifies a lot of your other spending.
- It's proof that there is a demand for your product or service.
- It's *one* of the key metrics for your business.
- It's a benchmark for growth.

How revenue is helpful:

Monitoring your revenue will help you create strategies to generate revenue, set monthly targets, predict cash flow, and determine where to focus your marketing spend. Tracking your monthly revenue is a must for every business owner.

2. Gross Profit

What it is:

Gross profit is also known as gross margin or income before expenses. It is revenue minus the direct costs associated with selling that product or service (e.g., direct labor, shipping).

Why gross profit is important:

- It's not about what you sell it for, it's what you get to keep.
- Allows you to assess pricing so you can improve profitability.

- Provides visibility to what it costs you to sell your product or service.
- Gross profit is the efficiency of your use of resources (labor, materials, etc.).

How gross profit is helpful:

This metric is extremely important to ensure pricing is profitable and resources are efficiently managed. If you are a service-based business, you may not have a lot of direct selling costs (cost of goods sold). It's okay to have a 100% gross profit percentage if no direct costs can be identified. Then you move on to focus on efficiency of your operations and ROI (return on investment) of other spending.

NOTE: Percentages are important! Like many businesses, you may experience fluctuating revenue and gross profit dollars. Looking at percentages can help you identify profit leaks. In other words, protect your margins!

Gross Profit $ Calculation: gross sales – cost of goods sold = gross profit $

Gross Profit % Calculation: gross profit $ / gross revenue $ = gross profit %

The higher your gross profit %, the better!

3. Burn Rate

What it is:

A burn rate is what it costs you to run your business even if you didn't sell a thing. It's the cash you burn through each month regardless of other activity.

Why burn rate is important:

- Knowing your burn rate means you know what your gross profit needs to be to break even during any given period.
- Allows you to set monthly sales targets for you and your team.
- Gives you a baseline cost for running your business.

How burn rate is helpful:

Analyzing your burn rate forces you to look at each expense so you can verify that each cost is necessary and in alignment for this next season of growth in your business.

Oftentimes, costs are more certain than revenue. Here is your first exercise to help you determine your monthly burn rate.

List all your recurring expenses that you would pay even if you didn't sell anything. Common examples are below:

- Software subscriptions: monthly and annual renewals (do not forget annual!)
- Workspace: coworking membership, rent or lease

- Payroll: for staff that isn't included in direct sale (meaning, they are paid regardless of what you sell)
- Vendor commitments: professional services like marketing, legal, accounting, insurance

Some expenses you'll want to use a twelve-month average for:

- Office supplies
- Travel
- Meals and entertainment

Once you have listed all your expenses including the averages, tally them up. This will be your average monthly burn rate! It will help you answer some very important questions coming later in this chapter.

4. Net Income

What it is:

Net income is also known as net profit or net earnings. It shows the company profit after taking all expenses into consideration.

Why net income is important:

Net income represents the profitability of your business. Consistent net income indicates a sustainable business, which is what we all want! It's important to note that net income on your Profit and Loss Statement may not include all your cash transactions, which is why this is only one of the five numbers you need to know.

How net income is helpful:

Your monthly net income indicates the financial health of your business. While it's likely to fluctuate, a positive net income trend is a good sign of a sustainable, scalable business assuming you are protecting the *queen* herself: cash.

5. Cash

What it is:

Cash = money in the bank! Your bank balance shows the cash you have on hand to use in your business. It's easily accessible, also called *liquid*, for you to use in your daily operations.

Looking at your cash balance by itself will not tell you the whole story. Maybe that cash is already set aside for outstanding payment obligations and therefore isn't really available.

Let's take it a step further. Your *cash flow* is the money that's flowing in and out of your business. Having a positive cash flow means that more money is coming in to the business than is going out. Cash flow is one of your most important numbers to track, monitor, and protect!

Why cash and cash flow are important:

Cash is the fuel for your business. Positive cash flow (more cash in than out) means you have more opportunities to invest in yourself and your business. Money always gives you choices!

How cash and cash flow are helpful:

Cash balances and cash flow projections are critical tools to help you make more confident financial decisions.

Here is a quick exercise to get started.

Exercise: Cash Flow Quickie

Create a cash flow projection for a "typical month" using the following format (paper or spreadsheet—you choose).

Columns: Day of month 1–9, 10–20, 21–EOM (end of month)

Rows:

Cash Inflow: List your projected monthly cash inflow here (monthly billing, recurring revenue, etc.).

Cash Outflow: List your projected monthly outflow (expenses) here based on when they are paid.

Net Cash Position Sum of Inflow/Outflow for each column 1–9, 10–20, 21–EOM (end of month)

Once you have the info above, you can clearly see where you can make improvements!

Inflows improvements:

- When are you billing clients each month?
- Have you set up auto ACH drafts or credit card authorizations to receive the money faster?

- How much more revenue do you need each month to create a positive cash flow position for the month? For each of the three columns?

Outflow improvements:

- When are your expenses coming out each month?
- Are you paying them when due? (DUE, not when received. No need to pay your bills early. Hi, Mom!)
- Can you move the due date to be more favorable to your cash flow? (Credit card due dates can be moved.)
- Can you cancel recurring expenses that no longer align with your current business model or goals?

Understanding your cash flow will help you make more confident financial decisions. Speaking of financial decisions, you know I love investing in myself and my business. I feel the greatest transformations and trajectories have come from betting on myself, so I must address some tips for you as it relates to this incredible subject.

Investing in Self or Business

Surely, you've made some. Investments may or may not be part of your burn rate (BR). If you hire someone that you pay on a recurring basis, that would be included in your BR until the agreement is complete. If you purchase a one-time course or mastermind, it would not; however, you will need to include these one-time investments in your cash flow projections.

Investing in self and business is a hot topic. In fact:

- This is one of the top questions I hear from business owners.
- This is a common mistake I see business owners make.
- This can be avoided if you follow the process below.

Four Things to Consider Before Making an Investment

1) What is it *costing* you not to do this? This may not be easy to quantify, but there is a cost associated with everything you say yes or no to.

- Time
- Stress
- Lack of sleep
- Poor decision-making
- Amateur output

Is the investment you're considering going to provide a solution that costs less than the *cost* of what you're doing today? (This is opportunity cost.)

2) What are the benefits—tangible, intangible?

- Knowledge
- Network
- Relationship
- Accountability
- Peace of mind
- Relief

3) Does your projected cash flow support this investment?

When do you believe you will recoup the investment, your ROI (return on investment)? When you invest time and money into something, you expect to get more time and money back.

- Will it give you your time back?
- Will it move the needle in your business? Example: someone selling on your behalf.
- Will it free up time for you to sell?
- Will it provide scalable strategy, accountability, visibility?

4) What are the success metrics for this investment? What would need to happen for you to feel like this was wildly successful?

Coming from someone who strongly believes in investing in self and resources for her business, I am all for it. In working with hundreds of entrepreneurs, I have identified some common pitfalls to share with you so you can avoid them:

- Investing, but not implementing.
- FOMO. Keepin' up with so-and-so who is further along.
- Lack of clarity around agreement, deliverables, time commitment.
- Not using time freed up to generate revenue.
- Investing in too many things at one time and being unable to capitalize on all of them.

You are going to come across many opportunities to invest in yourself and your business. Use the criteria above to help you make more confident decisions so you can clearly move forward with best possible outcomes.

Friends, money has a tendency to simply disappear if you aren't looking at it. You work hard for that cash. Show up for your money, and your money will show up for you!

How to Use Your Five Numbers

Once you understand your five numbers, you are equipped to answer some of the most common questions I get asked as a CFO:

Question #1: Am I profitable?

Your burn rate will allow you to set the monthly revenue and gross profit targets you need to reach in order to be profitable. Here is a quick illustration.

Let's say your monthly expenses are $15,000. You have no COGS (service based), and you owe $1,000 a month in debt obligation (to pay down a loan).

$15,000 monthly expenses + $1,000 loan paydown = $16,000 total monthly burn rate

In this simple example, anything you collect in gross profit for that month over $16,000 is net profit!

Question #2: How do I manage inconsistent cash flow?

If you know your burn rate, you will know how long your cash will last.

If you have $75,000 in your bank accounts and per the example above, your burn rate is $16,000, your cash will last you about 4.5 months ($75,000 cash / $16,000, BR/DO). Knowing your cash will cover you for 4.5 months doesn't mean you take your foot off the gas in selling, it means you become really intentional about what you're offering and when. Remember, when in doubt, generate revenue. Nobody wants to wake up, look in their bank account, and realize, "Oh shit, I have to go sell something ASAP." I call this a scarcity launch, and it happens often, but not to you because you are empowered and informed and now you know how long your cash will last.

Rule of thumb because I know you're thinking about it: Ideally, you should build up between three and six months of BR in your cash reserves. Many early-stage entrepreneurs do not have this (yet) but should be actively working toward it.

Question #3: How can I become more profitable?

Knowing your burn rate is one thing, but owning it is when you step into your true power.

I can't begin to tell you how many times we "free up" cash for people just by asking this simple question:

What are you spending money on that no longer supports your mission?

Do you really need that software subscription? Watch out for upcoming annual renewals and cancel, if not needed, prior to the charge. That coworking space that you use once every three months, is it worth the monthly investment? Is that contractor's performance exceeding expectations or, better yet, still in alignment with the direction of your company?

As you can see, your burn rate is powerful and owning it will empower you as the business owner.

BONUS: 5 x 5 x 5

5 ways to increase REVENUE

5 ways to become more PROFITABLE

5 ways to improve CASH FLOW

5 ways to increase REVENUE

- New clients: More paying clients, more revenue! Be mindful of you and your team's capacity in creating new client targets to make sure you hire support to scale without burning out.
- Price increases: Even a small price increase can have a big impact on your bottom line, assuming your costs have not increased the same.
- New offers: Determine other solutions you can bring to market for existing or new clients.
- Recurring revenue: Create programs that offer ongoing support so recurring revenue becomes part of your financial model.
- Passive income: Build it once, sell it forever! Evergreen courses, affiliate income, repurposing workshops are all ways to create passive income.

5 ways to become more PROFITABLE

- Increase pricing: Yes, here it is again. Pricing is a major contributor to overall profitability.
- Reduce costs: Where are the opportunities to reduce your costs while still delivering the same or better experience for your client?
- Create efficiencies: How can you and your team work smarter, faster, cheaper?
- Automate recurring tasks, streamline communication, set your team up for success, evaluate often.
- More value, less discounting: Offer a bonus or an add-on before you discount to protect your profit margins. Refer to pricing strategies to see how to effectively use discounting.
- Build merchant processing fees (estimated 3.5% as I write this) into your price so you are not fully responsible for these costs, especially for higher-ticket items.

5 ways to improve CASH FLOW

- Receive money faster: Set up electronic invoicing and payment receipts.
- Pay out money slower: Pay when bills are *due*, not when received.
- Use business credit cards (responsibly): Business credit cards can be a great tool to establish business credit (different from your own personal credit), buy time (debit cards hit directly to bank account, credit card payments are due monthly) and snag some rewards (points, miles, cash

back, etc.). The best credit card to use for your business? The one you'll pay off every month. :)
- Create recurring revenue offers so you have consistent cash inflow to cover your monthly cash outflow.
- Do not over-invest all at once: Too many entrepreneurs are investing in courses, masterminds, coaches all at the same time. If feeling aligned, pick one and go all in on the one that you feel will create the largest ROI (return on investment) and go for it.

Entrepreneurial Energy Check-In

This is a quick and easy way to check in with some key areas of your life, which I have broken down into five buckets as shown below.

Health	Mindset	Relationships	Finances	Fun
Active Nourished Rested Listening to your body	Connected Growth-oriented Solitude Rituals	Healthy Supportive Trust Honesty	Current Growing Empowered Expansive	Adventure Laughter Travel Play

For each of the five buckets, rank them on a scale of 0 to 5 where 0 is rock bottom and 5 is rock star.

1. Health. 0 1 2 3 4 5
2. Mindset. 0 1 2 3 4 5
3. Relationships. 0 1 2 3 4 5
4. Finances. 0 1 2 3 4 5
5. Fun. 0 1 2 3 4 5

This is a great exercise to do when heading into a new week. For any bucket ranking lower than the others, ask yourself these two questions:

- Why do I feel this way?
- What is one step I can take to improve it in the upcoming week?

Then add it to your calendar ASAP!

The best part? You now have the tools in this book for each of the five buckets to help you improve your ranking when one is feeling low. See correlation below:

Health, Mindset, Fun: Take a scan through your FMB list and put some of those in your calendar ASAP!

Relationships: Do a people inventory to see where you might have energy leaks and replace them with soul-filling, meaningful conversations.

Finances: Run through your offers, the five numbers, and your cash flow so you can get clear about what steps are needed to reach the next best outcome. Money is fluid. Find your financial flow!

CHAPTER 7
Rituals

Ritual defined: an act or series of acts regularly repeated in a set, precise manner.[15]

You have arrived at the most important part of this book. It doesn't matter how much knowledge you consume if you don't implement any of it.

Your finances are the results of your rituals. When you change your rituals, you change your results. Put simply, your behaviors matter.

Think back to a time where you achieved a goal. There was intentional action toward it. Luck had very little to do with it, right? You committed to rituals that allowed you to prevail.

As I write this book, I'm training for a marathon. While this isn't my first, it has been five years since I completed my last. I truly thought I was done with distance running forever. I had already run three full marathons and was no longer enjoying the process. I felt I had nothing to prove and didn't want to make the

---

[15] "ritual," *Merriam-Webster.com Dictionary,* Merriam-Webster, accessed June 15, 2023, https://www.merriam-webster.com/dictionary/ritual.

commitments required to get through the training program. So, I hung it up and released my identity as a person who runs marathons. I was still joining my running group for weekly three-to-four-mile runs and walks.

Then at the end of 2022, something changed. I felt intrigued by the concept of physically and emotionally challenging myself in that way again. *Could I possibly be considering this?* I mean, I'm older, wiser, and curvier! The fact that it was no longer a *hell no* had me wondering. So, I made a promise to myself. If I could get myself back up to running six miles by 12/31/22 (and not hate it!), I would register for another marathon. I completed my six miles, didn't hate it, and registered for a marathon in CA that same day. Update: I finished all 26.2 miles, and while I had some challenges, I still completed it in better time than my first marathon.

The act of running didn't change, my *perception* of it did. Once I established my goal of completing the marathon, running became my ritual. My repeatable activity that would get me closer to my goal. I saw it through a different lens and began to enjoy the challenge again.

Not every ritual has to be physically and emotionally challenging like training for a marathon, but in order to become a ritual, you have to be committed, consistent, and actively measuring change.

Every mile(stone) I reached in my training program got me closer to my goal.

Your business may not have a finish line like a marathon does (unless you plan to scale and sell!), but like a marathon, your business requires commitment, consistency, and measuring change.

Throughout this book, you have received my most sought-after strategies for running a profitable business while living a fuller life. Now I'm going to give you the exact framework to pull them all together into weekly and monthly rituals so you can easily implement what you have learned.

"Simplicity is the ultimate sophistication." —Leonardo da Vinci

Weekly Rituals

Pick a day that works best for you. I love to do this on a Sunday afternoon or a Monday morning to get myself ready for the week ahead.

Ritual #1:

Entrepreneurial Energy Check-In. (See page 91 Entrepreneurial Energy Check-In.)

Based on how I feel at this moment, how do I rank myself in each of the following buckets: Health, Mindset, Relationships, Finances, and Fun?

For any bucket ranking lower than the others, ask yourself these two questions:

- Why do I feel this way?
- What is one step I can take to improve it in the upcoming week?

Then add it to your calendar ASAP!

Ritual #2:

Cash Flow Check-In. Keep it simple in two steps. (See page 83 Cash Flow Quickie.)

1. Did you have more cash in or out for this past week?
   + Cash inflow for the week
   - Cash outflow for the week
   = Net Cash Position
2. What cash activity do I expect in the upcoming week and how can I plan for it?

Ritual #3:

Plan your week! Open your calendar and make some magic happen.

- What commitments are coming up? What do I need to prepare? Schedule time, as needed.
- If my goals include growing my business, do I have income-producing activities (IPAs) in my calendar?
- Add your focus areas uncovered by your Entrepreneurial Energy Check-In from Ritual #1. For example, say you ranked low in health. Schedule a walk or a workout. Just like any appointment, this is one you do not miss.
- Review your FMB list (See page 45 FMB List) to make sure you have some of those sprinkled in your week.

Your calendar is simply a documentation of rituals that create results in the form of money, joy, or both.

Monthly Rituals

Ritual #4: Monthly Money Date

This is your uninterrupted, sacred, quality time with your money! Now before you picture yourself in a bathtub filled with dollar bills, let me clarify what I mean below and then you can decide if a bathtub is part of your plan. It's your date!

I have clients and peers who wear an actual crown during this date, and it makes my heart smile every time I think about it.

1. Set up your space. Have fun with it. Light a candle. Play music. Pour yourself a beverage. Eliminate distractions. This is your time to honor your money.

2. Login to your systems. Make it easy on yourself. Before you get started, login to all the systems that make up your financial footprint. Your financial software, spreadsheets, tracking tools, bank accounts, credit cards, etc. Tip: Close all other windows and turn notifications off. Like any relationship, the one with your money deserves your attention.

3. Review your five numbers (See page 77 Five Numbers): revenue, gross profit, burn rate, net income, cash flow to see how they are tracking month over month. Questions to ask yourself:
    - What rituals created these results?
    - How do I feel about these results?

- What rituals can I change to produce the results I'm looking for?
    - Use your resources for offers, pricing and cash flow (See page 89, BONUS section 5x5x5).

4. Complete (or review) your Calendar Review for the last month. (See page 63 Calendar Review.) Questions to ask yourself:
    - What is my Calendar Review telling me about my priorities? Do they align with my goals?
    - Does my FMB list exist anywhere in my schedule?
    - What are the items in my Energy– column and how can I be sure to set better boundaries in the future?
    - What are the items in my Energy+ column and how can I be sure to schedule more of that ASAP?

5. Create a list of intentions for the next thirty days related to your energy, time, people, and money. Revisit your progress during your next monthly money date, if not before. Celebrate all shifts toward greater alignment and abundance.

With these weekly and monthly rituals, you will quickly begin to see how your revenue, resources, and rituals have you well on your way to a profitable business and a fuller life.

What to Do Next

Take a few big, deep breaths and honor yourself for picking up this book and completing the processes. Your curiosity converted into action! Bravo, queen.

Here are four ways to stay in flow with this energy:

1. Get your free resources.
   The resources in this book were carefully designed to make your journey easier and more fun. Go to https://bit.ly/moneyqueenresources to get all the free bonuses to accompany this book.

2. Book Bridgette to speak at your upcoming event.
   Ready to share this powerful message with your community? I'd love to bring this energy to your stage to help your audience begin their financial empowerment journey just like you did. Visit https://www.bridgetteboucha.com/speaking to start the conversation.

3. Hire the Financial Unicrowns CFO team.
   Get started with our signature Money Mapping Experience, packed with virtual and in-person strategy

sessions to get you clarity around your numbers and deliver a roadmap to reach your goals. Submit your application at https://www.bridgetteboucha.com/money-mapping-session.

4. Connect on social.

Let's stay connected so we can continue this journey together. Follow @bridgetteboucha and @financialunicrowns on Instagram to make it happen. Shoot me a DM to let me know you're there.

Hugs, High Fives, and Cheers,
Your Soulful CFO Bridgette

Acknowledgments

MIKE: I'd like to thank my husband for riding this roller coaster with me, never once threatening to jump off. Being married to an entrepreneur who went from dreamer to doer is not always easy, but you allow me the space to do my thing and love me through it all. Buckle up, honey . . . more to come!

MOM: I'd like to thank my mom for demonstrating what female financial empowerment and independence can look like, no matter what situation you find yourself in. Your unwavering love and support have been foundational as I continue to define, experience, and celebrate my biggest, juiciest, most joyful life.

DAD: I'd like to thank my dad for showing me that you can achieve incredible things regardless of your circumstances. Adversity can create opportunities when met with determination and talent. Your vision to serve, speak, and write along with my years of cleaning, mowing, and slinging breakfast plates have certainly been a catalyst in my entrepreneurial spirit.

AMANDA: I'd like to thank Amanda, my business partner and co-founder of Financials Unicrowns. You make everything more FUN. Your encouragement and support of me writing this book during a crazy-busy time in our business is just one example of the love you have in your heart and the gift you are to this world. Pew Pew Pew. Crown up!

BARB & MITCHELL: I'd like to thank my in-laws, Barb and Mitchell, for living their most adventurous lives and allowing me to be part of some truly incredible experiences. You play a big role in me fulfilling CFO, seaFO, skiFO responsibilities, and I appreciate and love you both for it.

CHRIS & LORI HARDER: I'd like to thank Chris and Lori for creating the room that would become my very first mastermind. Your commitments to personal growth, dedication to massive service, and passion for witty one-liners have added so much joy and inspiration to my life. I appreciate your friendship, mentorship, and support.

ROB & KIM MURGATROYD: I'd like to thank Rob and Kim for designing the most incredible experiences for entrepreneurs like me who needed exactly what you have to offer. Not only do you live a fuller life, by design, but you were an instrumental boost for getting this book into the world. GRAZIE!

JAKE KELFER: I'd like to thank Jake for being an incredible book coach and mentor. Without his expertise and guidance, you'd be holding someone else's book right now. Cannot thank you enough for helping first-time authors like me get our messages from head to paper and into the hands of those who need it most.

KAREN HUGHES: I'd like to thank Karen for being the woman who first made me a CFO, Chief Financial Officer. Your belief in me gave me a gift that keeps on giving. I'm forever grateful for the lessons, laughter, and continued support after all these years.

COMMUNITY: I'd like to thank my people! My running/workout groups who have listened to my dreams for many years over several miles and through lots of coffee chats. My Warroad besties who have shown unconditional love and support for every version of me that has existed to date. My college besties who always pick up right where we left off, often resulting in the best belly laughs that soothe the soul. My entrepreneurial family, whom without your support, I would not be having nearly as much fun as I am today!

QUEEN: I'd like to thank YOU for choosing this book. You deserve all the best life has to offer. Make money, make memories, and make NO apologies for either one!

Would Love to Hear From You!

If you're enjoying this book and the resources provided have brought you value, please take a few moments to write a review wherever you bought this book. So many entrepreneurs are struggling because they lack clarity and confidence around their numbers. Without this simple framework, they may end up burned out and leaving their mission behind. Taking a few moments to share your honest feedback may be the catalyst in helping someone else receive this message. Financial empowerment looks good on everyone. Join the Money Queen movement by writing a review today!

Massive love and appreciation for you!

Bridgette Boucha (boo-shay) is a speaker, writer, and fractional CFO who advises from her lived experiences as an entrepreneur. Not only did she start and scale her own multi-six-figure business during a viral pandemic, but she continues to help multi-six- and seven-figure entrepreneurs develop financial strategies to reach their unique goals. Her soulful approach to money mentorship and personal empowerment has helped hundreds of business owners simplify their money, build confidence in their numbers, and map out their profitable business, fuller life model. She believes you deserve to get the most out of your life and business and does her best to live it as a lover of all things travel, wine, and belly laughs. Connect with Bridgette on social @bridgetteboucha.

Made in the USA
Monee, IL
26 August 2023

41656925R00069